These are all hippos.

Hippos are big animals

This hippo is as big as a car.

A baby hippo is little.

This baby hippo is
as little as a dog.

Hippos live here.

They like to live by water.

Hippos like to live
with lots of hippos.

This is a hippo family.

The sun is up.

It is hot.
The mother hippo is hot.

The mother hippo
gets in the water.

In the water, it is not so hot.

The baby hippo is hot.

The baby hippo wants to go in the water.

The baby hippo is too little.

The baby hippo gets
on the mother hippo.

This is mud.

The hippos get in the mud.

The mud stops the sun.

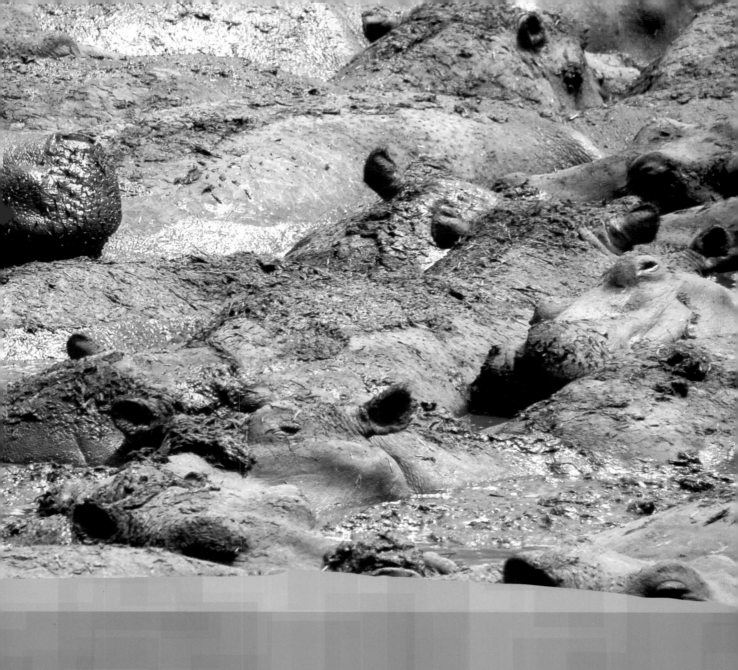

The crocodile is
in the water, too.

The crocodile wants to get the baby hippo.

Look at the mother
hippo's big mouth.

Look at her big teeth.

She will not let the crocodile get her baby.

The mother hippo will fight the crocodile.

Now the crocodile will go away.

The mother and her
baby are safe.

The sun is down. The hippos get out of the water.

Now all the hippos go to sleep.

HIPPO FACTS

The word hippo is short for hippopotamus.

The teeth of hippos can grow to 20 inches in length.

Hippos live for about 45 years.

A baby hippo is called a calf.

The hippo is one of the heaviest land animals along with the elephant and rhinoceros. It can weigh up to 8,000 pounds!

A group of hippos is called a herd, bloat, or crash.

Hippos actually can't swim or float. They move around underwater by pushing off of the bottom of the river or walking along the riverbed.

Hippos can hold their breath for an average of 5 minutes at a time. Their ears and nostrils automatically close as they go underwater.

HIPPO ANATOMY

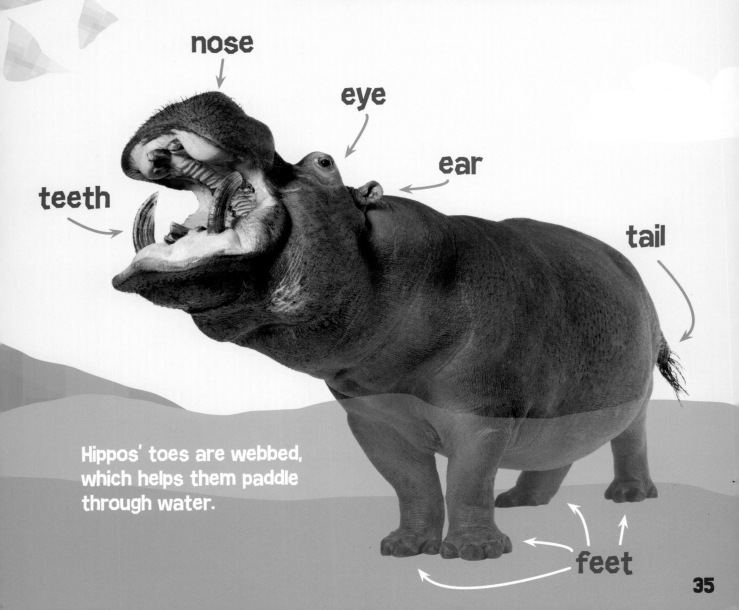

nose

eye

ear

teeth

tail

Hippos' toes are webbed, which helps them paddle through water.

feet

POWER WORDS

a	get	lots	they
all	go	mother	this
and	her	not	to
animal	here	now	too
are	in	of	up
as	is	on	want
at	it	out	will
baby	like	she	with
big	little	stop	
by	live	the	
family	look	these	

This is a hippo.

HIPPO MOMS

Matt Reher   Katie Axt